Totally Lent!

A KID'S JOURNEY TO EASTER 2008

Sr. Alice Ann Pfeifer, CSA

Pflaum Publishing Group
Dayton, OH 45439

About the Author

Sr. Alice Ann Pfeifer, CSA, is a teacher, writer, and student. She has a B.A. in English from Marian College, Fond du Lac, WI; an M.A. in English from Marquette University, Milwaukee, WI; and is currently working toward an M.A. in pastoral studies in the distance education program from St. Joseph's College in Standish, ME. She lives, writes, and studies in her hometown of Hays, KS.

Edited by Jean Larkin
Cover and interior illustration by Doug Jones, www.dougjonesart.com
Graphic design by Kathryn Cole

ISBN 978-1-933178-71-4

My Lenten Prayer

Dear Jesus, here I am on my Lenten journey.
Please keep me strong and faithful.
I want to try really hard to pray,
to sacrifice, and to serve others.

When you were in the desert for forty days,
you got tired and hungry.
The devil tried hard to make you
take the easy way out.
The devil wanted you to choose darkness instead of light.

But you wouldn't give in.
You kept your mind on your goal.
You followed your own plan.
You showed me that even when something is hard,
it can be done.
I can be faithful because you were,
and you are always with me.

So walk with me throughout these forty days.
Help me do what you did.
You stayed faithful.
You stayed strong.
You never forgot your goal.

I ask this in your name,
for I know that you will always
help me when I ask. Amen.

This book belongs to

_____

Looking Up the Daily Gospel

At the top of almost every page in this book, you will find a Bible reference for that day's Gospel. For instance, on Ash Wednesday, you will see the reference, Matthew 6:1-6, 16-18.

The Bible consists of 73 small books all gathered together to make one big book. Each small book has its own title. The four Gospel books are Matthew, Mark, Luke, and John.

A Bible reference has three parts:
1. The name of the book in the Bible
2. The number for the chapter in that book
3. One or more numbers for the verses in that chapter

Here is how to look up the Bible reference for Ash Wednesday's Gospel: Matthew 6:1-6, 16-18.

Matthew—Find *Matthew* in the table of contents at the front of your Bible. Then go to the page where this Gospel starts.

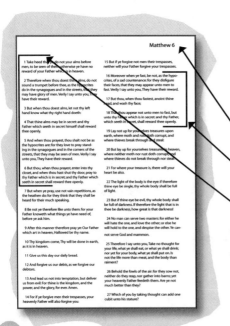

6—Matthew's Gospel has 28 chapters in all, but this number shows that you should go to chapter 6.

1-6, 16-18—Every chapter has numbered verses. These numbers show that you should look for verses 1-6 and 16-18.

Walking with Jesus

Lent consists of the forty days (excluding Sundays) that come before Easter. On February 6 this year, we begin a forty-day walk with Jesus. We pray and fast to show sorrow for our sins and to imitate Jesus, who prepared for his public life with forty days of prayer and fasting.

Jesus came among us as a man on a mission. He wanted to prove God's love for every single human being on earth—past, present, and yet to be born. Even if only one human being had ever existed—*you*—Jesus still would have come to earth with his message of love. He still would have lived and died just for *you*.

The Gospels tell the good news about the life, death, and resurrection of Jesus. Those who follow Jesus love hearing and reading about him. They reread the Gospels the way families tell the same stories, over and over, about family members and events.

If you read from this book each day during Lent, by Easter Sunday you will feel closer to Jesus than before. You will know what it's like to walk and talk with him every day.

Plan ahead!

Make a centerpiece for your family's Easter dinner table or a favor for each person who shares your Easter dinner. See page 43 to learn about Easter grass and how to grow your own.

Today's Gospel: Matthew 6:1-6, 16-18

"Beware of practicing your piety before others so they will see you; for then you have no reward from your Father in heaven" (6:1).

Jesus talks about three ways of practicing piety—ways we still practice today. He says it is very important to do them right.

Take this Piety Quiz to see if you remember what he says.

Almsgiving means giving your time or treasure to someone who needs it. When you do this, Jesus says not to sound a trumpet (6:2). **What does he mean?**

____ Don't blow a horn when putting money in the offering basket.
____ Don't help others just for show.

Praying is talking with God. Jesus says not to stand and pray on street corners but to pray behind closed doors (6:5-6). **What does he mean?**

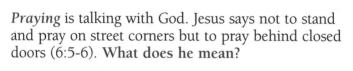

____ Don't pray outdoors.
____ Don't pray just so other people will think you are holy.

Fasting means *giving up* something you really like as a way of *giving back* to God. It can be anything: candy, TV, etc. When you fast, Jesus says to fast in secret (6:18). **What does he mean?**

____ Don't fast unless you can keep it a secret from every one you know.
____ Don't fast to show people how good you are. Fast to show God your love.

Today's Gospel: Luke 9:22-25

"If any want to become my followers, let them deny themselves and take up their cross daily and follow me" (9:23).

To take up your cross means to accept cheerfully the hard things in your life. Almsgiving, prayer, and fasting can be hard.

*Here are some crosses you might pick up for Lent. Are they examples of Almsgiving, Praying, or Fasting? Identify each with an **A**, a **P**, or an **F**.*

1. Take out the garbage without being told. _____

2. Tell God you're sorry when you do wrong. _____

3. Skip the candy at the movies. _____

4. Don't watch a favorite TV show. _____

5. Buy a friend a treat. _____

6. Say a rosary. _____

7. Give your allowance to a food bank. _____

8. Help your brother with his homework. _____

9. Keep silent when you feel like talking back. _____

10. Ask for God's help on a test. _____

11. Don't play video games. _____

12. Talk to God on the way to school. _____

What *one* good thing will you try to do every day between now and Easter? Write it here. It will be your Lenten resolution—a promise between you and God.

Today's Gospel: Matthew 9:14-15

John's disciples asked Jesus, "Why do we and the Pharisees fast often, but your disciples do not fast?" Jesus explained: "The wedding guests cannot mourn as long as the bridegroom is with them, can they?" (9:14-15)

Jesus knew he was like the groom at a wedding feast. His followers were like the guests. At a wedding, people eat, drink, and have a good time. They don't fast.

But Jesus also knew that one day he would be killed. On that day, his disciples would be too sad to eat or drink. On that day, they would fast. During Lent we think about how Jesus died to save us from sin and death, and we feel sad. We express sorrow for our sins.

Can you find these 12 sins in this Word Search?

Curse	Hurt	Brag	Lie
Talk Back	Skip Mass	Fight	Cheat
Steal	Disobey	Envy	Bully

F	M	C	H	E	A	T	K	P
V	S	K	E	R	Y	C	N	D
E	K	Q	I	H	A	V	I	C
S	I	B	L	B	U	S	N	T
R	P	U	K	B	O	R	N	E
U	M	L	M	B	W	R	T	N
C	A	L	E	V	G	A	R	B
T	S	Y	T	H	G	I	F	L
Q	S	L	S	T	E	A	L	N

Today's Gospel: Luke 5:27-32

Jesus asked Levi, a tax collector, to follow him. Levi left everything and followed Jesus. Then Levi gave a great banquet for Jesus and invited other tax collectors. People questioned this by asking Jesus, "Why do you eat and drink with tax collectors and sinners?" (5:27-30)

At that time, most tax collectors were cheats and thieves. No wonder people were shocked that Jesus would socialize with them. They thought Jesus should only be with good people.

Find out what Jesus told the people. Complete these sentences based on today's Gospel by filling in the missing vowels, A, E, I, O, or U.

TH___ S___ WH___ ___R___ W___LL D___ N___T

N___ ___D ___ D___CT___R. ___NLY S___CK

P___ ___PL___ D___. ___ H___V___ C___M___ N___T

T___ C___LL G___ ___D P___ ___PL___ B___T T___

C___LL S___NN___RS.

Your Weekly Checkup

Last Thursday, you made a Lenten resolution. Now it's time to ask yourself some questions.

1. What have you done this week to keep your resolution?

_____

_____

2. Are you happy with what you have done? Why or why not?

_____

_____

What's THAT about?

In church on every Ash Wednesday, you are signed on the forehead with ashes. Why ashes instead of, say, holy water?

In ancient times, God's people showed sorrow for sin by doing two things. They wore sackcloth, and they covered themselves with ashes. Sackcloth is a rough fabric made from the same thing as heavy rope. (Ouch! You've heard of rope burns, haven't you?) People made themselves feel itchy with sackcloth and dirty with ashes on purpose. They wanted their action to be a prayer. This prayer said, "Inside, I feel itchy and dirty because of my sins. Lord, have mercy."

Today we no longer wear sackcloth to show sorrow for sin. But on one day a year, we do wear ashes.

Walking with Jesus

Prayer and fasting are ways to show love for God. Almsgiving is a way to show love for the needy. Sometimes the needy are right in your own home. They are in your school, your parish, your neighborhood.

Look at these examples. Match each person with the best action that you could take to help him or her.

1. ___ Mom

2. ___ Dad

3. ___ Bored little kid

4. ___ Hurt little kid

5. ___ Teacher

6. ___ Bullied classmate

7. ___ Lonely classmate

8. ___ Sick classmate

9. ___ Elderly shut-in

10. ___ Stranger at Mass

11. ___ Overseas soldier or missionary

12. ___ Deceased relative

A. Let the teacher know about the bully.

B. Pray for his or her eternal rest.

C. Help with keeping the classroom clean.

D. Help with keeping up with missed schoolwork.

E. Help with yard work

F. Play some fun and simple games with him or her.

G. Offer a sincere handshake of peace, and smile.

H. Write a letter to thank him or her for serving.

I. Give him or her a band-aid and a hug.

J. Offer to run an errand that he or she cannot easily do.

K. During recess offer a few kind words and a smile.

L. Help with housework.

Today's Gospel: Matthew 25:31-46

"When the Son of Man comes in his glory...then he will sit on the throne of his glory" (25:31).

"He will come again in glory to judge the living and the dead...." You say this sentence every Sunday when you say the creed during Mass. But what really will happen on the last day? Today Jesus answers that question with a story.

Here is part of the story. Sometimes a picture is given instead of a word. See if you can guess the right word for the picture.

When the Son of Man comes with all his ![ghost], he will sit on his throne of glory. All nations will gather before him. Then he will separate them, as a ![shepherd] separates his ![sheep] from his goats. The ![sheep] he will put on his right ![hand] and the goats on his left.

The ![crown] will say to those on his right, "Come, you are blessed by my Father. You may enter my kingdom. For I was hungry and you gave me ![food], I was thirsty and you gave me ![glass of water]. I was a stranger and you welcomed me. I was naked and you gave me ![clothes]. I was sick and you took care of me. I was in ![jail] and you visited me."

Then these good people will say to him, "Lord, when was it that we ![saw] you hungry and gave you ![food]? **R** thirsty and gave you ![glass]? When were you a stranger and we welcomed you? **R** naked and gave you ![clothes]? When were you sick **R** in ![jail] and we visited you?"

And the ![crown] will answer them, "Whenever you did it to anyone, you did it to me. ![1] all human beings are members of my ![family]."

Today's Gospel: Matthew 6:7-15

"When you are praying, do not heap up empty phrases as the Gentiles do; for they think that they will be heard because of their many words" (6:7).

When you pray, do you think about the words you say? Or do you just pile up words? Right now, pray the Our Father slowly and thoughtfully. Stop often to reflect. Use this guide to help you.

Our Father, who art in heaven,
> *Picture the most perfect father you can imagine.*

hallowed be thy name;
> *Picture all the saints and angels bowing at God's name.*

thy kingdom come;
> *Imagine a perfect world, where love rules.*

thy will be done on earth as it is in heaven.
> *Think of how you will do God's will today.*

Give us this day our daily bread;
> *Think of all that you will need today. Ask God for it.*

and forgive us our trespasses as we forgive those who trespass against us;
> *Think of one person you need to forgive. Pray for that person.*

and lead us not into temptation, but deliver us from evil.
> *Think of one evil that concerns you. Picture God keeping you safe from it. Picture God's arms around you.*

Now circle your favorite part of the Our Father. On the lines below, put that part in your own words.

_____

_____

_____

_____

_____

_____

Today's Gospel: Luke 11:29-32

"This generation is an evil generation; it asks for a sign, but no sign will be given it except the sign of Jonah" (11:29).

Remember, Jonah was the prophet who spent three days in the belly of a whale. Then the whale spat him out upon the shore, and Jonah was fine and healthy. Jesus knew that soon he would die. He would spend three days in a grave. Then he would rise from the dead. All the people wanting a miracle *now* would just have to *wait.*

Do you sometimes want too much? What if, every time you wanted something, you gave something instead? Try it by finishing these sentences.

1. You want Mom or Dad to hurry up and get dinner on the table. You say:

   " Shall I set the table? "

2. You feel like yelling at a slowpoke who is holding you up. You say:

   " **"**

3. You wait a long time for a ride. When the driver comes, you say:

   " **"**

4. You feel let down because God did not answer your prayer the way you hoped. You tell God:

   " **"**

5. Your parents won't let you have something you want. You say:

   " **"**

Today's Gospel: Matthew 7:7-12

"If you then...know how to give good gifts to your children, how much more will your Father in heaven give good things to those who ask him!" (7:11)

Jesus told us today what a good father his own Father is. To learn more of what Jesus said, you'll have to solve these riddles first.

1 Think hard, for here's the hitch: I am two parts of every sandwich. _____

2 The saying goes that throwing this could break my knee, but words could never hurt me. _____

3 Catch me if you can, but you need a pole. I'll meet you at the swimming hole. _____

4 I slither around and make some people scream, but I really am not as bad as I seem. _____

Now, using the riddle answers in order, complete the quote from Jesus.

"Is there anyone among you who, if your child asks for

_____, *will give a* _____? *Or if the child asks*

for a _____, *will give a* _____?" **(7:9-10)**

Today is St. Valentine's Day! Do something loving for someone.

Today's Gospel: Matthew 5:20-26

"But I say to you that if you are angry with a brother or a sister, you will be liable to judgment" (5:22).

Jesus wasn't totally against fighting. After all, he fought for the poor and the weak. He fought for the kingdom of God. But Jesus was totally against a stupid fight. Today Jesus says to stay out of stupid fights and resist slinging insults or calling people names. He says we are still responsible for our actions even if we are angry.

Anger means "extreme displeasure." Whenever we let our anger become extreme, we do and say stupid things. Lighten things up a bit with this little rhyming exercise.

Fill the blanks with "anger" words that rhyme with the person's name, like in the example.

1. Don't **kill** Jill.

2. Don't _____ Burt.

3. Don't _____ Hank.

4. Don't _____ Sis.

5. Don't _____ Kate.

6. Don't _____ Father.

7. Don't _____ Doc.

8. Don't _____ Doug.

9. Don't _____ Britt.

10. Don't _____ Dwight.

11. Don't _____ Rick.

12. Don't _____ Lester.

Today's Gospel: Matthew 5:43-48

"You have heard that it was said, 'You shall love your neighbor and hate your enemy.' But I say to you, Love your enemies and pray for those who persecute you" (5:43-44).

---

1 *In the center chamber of this heart, write the initials of two people you love very much.*

2 *In the next chamber, write the initials of two people you like a lot.*

3 *In the outer chamber, write the initials of two people you like at least a little bit.*

4 *Finally, around the outside of the heart, write the initials of two people you don't like at all.*

To follow today's Gospel, try praying for someone who is *outside* your heart. Picture that person in your mind. Try to see at least *some* good in him or her.

Your Weekly Checkup

For almost two weeks, you have been working on a Lenten resolution. How well have you done?

1. On a scale of 1-10, how would you rate yourself? _____

Your Patron Saint

If you are having trouble remembering or keeping your resolution, ask your patron saint to help you. Your patron saint is one who prays especially for you. Every Catholic has one. If you know who your patron saint is, write his or her name here.

_____

Usually your patron saint has the same name as you. For example, if your name is Joe or Jo, then St. Joseph is your patron saint. Sometimes your patron saint has a feast day that falls on your birthday. For example, if you were born on March 17, St. Patrick is your patron saint. (This is true even if your name is not Patrick or Patricia.)

Do you want to know which saint was born on your birthday? Go to this page on the American Catholic web site.

www.americancatholic.org/features/saints/bydate.asp

Read about your saint. Then write three interesting facts you have learned about him or her.

1 _____

2 _____

3 _____

Peter Who?

This coming week, there are two Peters to celebrate. St. Peter Damian's feast day is Thursday, the 21st, and St. Peter the Apostle's feast day is Friday, the 22nd. So, if your name is Peter, you can celebrate twice this week!

There are a number of web sites on which you can read about many saints. Here are just three of them.

www.americancatholic.org
(click on Saint of the Day, then Patron Saints)
www.catholic-forum.com
(click on Patron Saints)
www.catholic.org
(click on Saints and Angels)

Take this little quiz to see how well you know which Peter is which. If you don't know an answer, check out one of those web sites.

Decide to which "Peter" each sentence refers and put a checkmark beneath his name.	Peter the Apostle	Peter Damian
1. I was an orphan and forced to herd pigs by my brother.		
2. I was the first bishop of Rome.		
3. I am a Doctor of the Church.		
4. I was a Benedictine monk.		
5. I witnessed Jesus' Transfiguration.		
6. I was a fisherman.		
7. I was appointed many times to represent the pope in various disputes.		
8. I denied knowing Jesus three times.		
9. I was called Simon until Jesus renamed me Peter.		
10. I wrote some of the best Latin of my time.		

Today's Gospel: Luke 6:36-38

"Do not judge, and you will not be judged; do not condemn, and you will not be condemned. Forgive, and you will be forgiven; give, and it will be given to you" (6:37-38).

Today's Gospel makes the point, "What goes around, comes around!" If you send love into the world, love comes back to you. If you send hate, hate comes back to you.

Read this story. You will have to supply the ending. Try to show that what goes around, comes around.

Saturday afternoon, Will planned to go to the mall. There was a new movie he really wanted to see, and his friends were all going.

In the kitchen, his mother was unhappy. "All these dishes," she said, "and I have to get to the grocery store and the pharmacy today for sure. I don't see how I'm going to get it all done!"

Will's first thought was to get out of the house fast before his mom asked him to do the dishes. But he also felt kind of sorry for his mother. He said,

_____

_____

_____

_____

With your ending, what did you send around that will come back to you?

_____

Today's Gospel: Matthew 23:1-12

"The greatest among you will be your servant" (23:11).

Jesus made it clear that being smart or talented or successful did not make a person GREAT. Being smart, talented, and successful is good as long as you don't get a big head and think you are better than others. Jesus said really GREAT people serve others. They do not expect others to serve them.

Are you ever guilty of acting like one of the Pharisees Jesus talked about today—making yourself more important than you really are?

Read each of these scenarios. A possible Pharisee reaction is given. You fill in how you would act if you were a GREAT person.

Scenario	Pharisee	GREAT Person
An elderly woman holds up the checkout line to count her change.	Sigh, roll your eyes, and mumble about being in a hurry.	
You see a friend farther ahead in a long ticket line.	Cut in front of your friend. After all, that's what friends are for.	
Cans of soup have fallen in the aisle at the store.	Walk around them. Someone else is paid to pick them up.	
A cake is cut for the guests to share.	Take the biggest piece.	

Today's Gospel: Matthew 20:17-28

"Whoever wishes to be great among you must be your servant, and whoever wishes to be first among you must be your slave" (20:26-27).

A big argument started among the apostles when the mother of James and John asked Jesus to put her boys in the places of greatest honor after he became king. Well, the other apostles resented this. *Everyone* wanted the greatest places. When Jesus overheard all the arguing, he must have thought, "How many times do I have to tell these guys what greatness is all about?"

Which of the following messages had Jesus given his apostles that meant the same thing he said today? Circle the letter of the best answer.

A "You have heard that it was said, 'You shall love your neighbor and hate your enemy.' But I say to you, Love your enemies and pray for those who persecute you" (Matthew 5:43-44).

B "When you are praying, do not heap up empty phrases as the Gentiles do; for they think that they will be heard because of their many words" (Matthew 6:7).

C "Whoever becomes humble like this child is the greatest in the kingdom of heaven" (Matthew 18:4).

D "If you then, who are evil, know how to give good gifts to your children, how much more will your Father in heaven give good things to those who ask him!" (Matthew 7:11)

E "But I say to you that if you are angry with a brother or sister, you will be liable to judgment" (Matthew 5:22).

Today's Gospel: Luke 16:19-31

Jesus told this story today. See if you can fill in the missing words. The first letter of each word is given to help you.

Once there was a rich man who feasted every **d**_____. At his gate lay a poor man named Lazarus, who was covered with **s**_____. Lazarus was so hungry that he gladly would have eaten scraps from the rich man's **t**_____. After Lazarus died, he was carried away to the side of **A**_____ in heaven. The rich man also died but he went to hell. When the rich man looked up and saw Lazarus in **h**_____, he begged Abraham for mercy. "Send Lazarus to dip his finger in water to touch my tongue. I am burning **u**___!" Abraham said, "Child, during your lifetime you had all good **t**_____ and Lazarus had none. Now, between you and him is a great **d**_____. No one can pass from one side to the **o**_____."

The rich man then begged, "Send Lazarus to warn my five **b**_____." Abraham said, "They have Moses and the prophets to warn **t**_____. If they do not listen to **M**_____ and the **p**_____, they will not be convinced even if someone rises from the **d**_____."

26 The Chair of St. Peter— February 22

Today's Gospel: Matthew 16:13-19

"And I tell you, you are Peter, and on this rock I will build my church, and the gates of Hades will not prevail against it" (16:18).

How would you like to be compared to a rock? That depends, doesn't it? No one wants to be called as dumb as a rock, but what if someone says you are as solid and as reliable as a rock? Now that's different. And that's exactly what Jesus told Peter.

Have you ever noticed the funny ways we compare ourselves to animals? Finish each sentence with the correct word or phrase.

1. You're as blind as a _____.

2. I'm as proud as a _____.

3. You're as ugly as a _____.

4. I'm as busy as a _____.

5. You're as big as an _____.

6. I'm as hungry as a _____.

7. You're as loose as a _____.

8. I'm as stubborn as a_____.

9. You're as sneaky as a _____.

10. I'm as clumsy as an _____.

Today, pray that you, too, might become as solid in your faith as Peter was in his.

Today's Gospel: Luke 15:1-3, 11-32
"There was a man who had two sons" (15:11).

Today Jesus tells the familiar story of the father and his two sons. The younger son runs off with his share of his father's money, spends it all foolishly, and comes home begging his father to take him back. Because the father loves him very much he is thrilled to see his younger son. He throws a big welcome-home party, which irritates his older son who stayed home and worked hard.

You might think this is just an old story about a foolish son and the mistakes he made. But it is really a story that can be told today, and it is about both sons.

*If you have ever said any of these things to your mother or father, which son (or daughter) were you being? Use a **Y** for the younger and an **O** for the older.*

1. "Leave me alone. I can do it myself." _____

2. "You always let her have her way." _____

3. "I'm old enough to make my own decisions." _____

4. "Why do I have to do all the work around here?" _____

5. "It's not fair!" _____

Whom does the father represent in the story? _____

Your Weekly Checkup

Which day this past week was your *best* day for keeping your resolution?

_____

Why was that day best?

_____

The Point of the Story

When Jesus told a story, he always made a point or taught a lesson. Let's look back at two of his stories we heard this week. Then you can make a point in a story of your own.

The Story of the Lost Son
Read again about the father and sons in the story Jesus told in Luke 15:1-3, 11-32 (page 25). What point was Jesus trying to make?

_____

From these possible answers, all except one are correct. Cross out the incorrect one.

A. Envy has no place in a loving heart.

B. Count your blessings.

C. God the Father is always ready to forgive.

D. God is always more than fair.

E. God loves sinners more than other people.

Walking with Jesus

The Story of Lazarus and the Rich Man

Now read again the story of Lazarus and the rich man on page 23. What do you think was the point Jesus was making in this story?

From these possible answers, all except one are correct. Cross out the incorrect one.

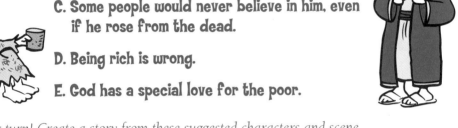

A. There really is a heaven and a hell.

B. The "haves" must share with the "have-nots."

C. Some people would never believe in him, even if he rose from the dead.

D. Being rich is wrong.

E. God has a special love for the poor.

Your turn! Create a story from these suggested characters and scene.
Characters: fifth-grade soccer team; two first-graders
Scene: the practice field

The Story of _____

_____

_____

_____

_____

_____

_____

_____

_____

 What's Your Point? _____

_____

Today's Gospel: Luke 4:24-30

"Truly I tell you. No prophet is accepted in the prophet's hometown" (4:24).

Jesus went to Nazareth, his hometown. The people there knew he had worked miracles in other towns. Surely, *now* he would work miracles for them.

Instead, Jesus stood up to preach. The people got angry, and mumbled, "Who is he to preach to us? We've known him all his life. Who does he think he is?" They got so angry they ran him out of town, planning to push him off a cliff.

Circle every fourth word in each row to find out what Jesus did.

I you she he it they

preached worked wondered passed understood

left center up right down over

in out over through under across

this that those the these an

outside inside overhead midst edge underground

with without about of in at

me you him them her us

but for or and nor neither either

saw took did went thought hoped

in under over on along around

its their her his our your

own mountain boat way medicine donkey

Today's Gospel: Matthew 18:21-35

Peter asked Jesus, "Lord, if another member of the church sins against me, how often should I forgive? As many as seven times?" (18:21)

Peter must have known some pesky people. Don't we all? They borrow things without returning them. They spread unkind stories about others. They laugh when others make mistakes. And they might do these things over and over. Do you have to forgive them over and over? Exactly how many times should you forgive someone?

To learn the number Jesus told Peter, follow these directions.

A Multiply 7 times 7. _____

B Add 50 to the number you got in A. _____

C Divide by 3 the number you got in B. _____

D Subtract 22 from the number you got in C. _____

E Multiply by 7 the number you got in D. _____

The answer to **E** is the number Jesus told Peter. At that time, that number stood for *infinity*, which means "forever and ever."

Certain numbers mean certain things for us, too. Can you fill in each blank with the right number?

Sweet _____

Terrible _____s

Lucky _____

Unlucky_____

A perfect _____

Loneliest number _____

Today's Gospel: Matthew 5:17-19

"Do not think that I have come to abolish the law or the prophets; I have come not to abolish but to fulfill" (5:17-18).

Sometimes Jesus confused people. He told them things they had never heard before, such as, "Love your enemies," and "Forgive one another endlessly." These were all completely new commands to them. So, people started getting the wrong idea. They thought the *old* commandments—the ones God gave Moses—didn't matter anymore.

Today Jesus sets the record straight. He says that *all* God's commandments, old and new, are important. Those who keep them will be great in heaven. Those who do not will be least.

Below are some of the Ten Commandments. Match each one with a way of breaking it. (If you don't understand an answer, ask an adult about it.)

___ 1. Do not take the Lord's name in vain.

___ 2. Keep the Lord's Day holy.

___ 3. Honor your father and mother.

___ 4. Do not kill.

___ 5. Do not steal.

___ 6. Do not lie.

A Spread unkind rumors about someone.

B Hit someone in anger.

C Yell "Jesus Christ!" in hurt, anger, or surprise.

D Copy another's answers on a test.

E Skip Sunday Mass.

F Complain when a parent gives you work to do.

Today's Gospel: Luke 11:14-23

"Every kingdom divided against itself becomes a desert....If Satan also is divided against himself, how will his kingdom stand?" (11:17-18)

Jesus had cured a mute—someone who cannot speak. When the mute started talking, nearly all were amazed. Some people, however, grumbled, "Jesus gets his power from the devil."

Jesus pointed out that the devil only does bad things, so why would he suddenly do something good? He would be working against himself.

Everyone is either on Jesus' team or on Satan's. Whose team are *you* on?

Complete these pictures. On the left, finish the figure as yourself—a member of God's team. Then, just for fun, on the right, show a player on the devil's team. Make that player really ugly!

Wise • Brave • Patient
Kind • Generous • Modest
Truthful • Faithful

Foolish • Cowardly • Cruel
Rash • Selfish • Boastful
Dishonest • Doubtful

Today's Gospel: Mark 12:28-34

Someone asked, "Which commandment is the first of all?" Jesus answers: "The first is, 'You shall love the Lord your God with all your heart, and with all your mind, and with all your strength.' The second is this, 'You shall love your neighbor as yourself' " (12:29-31).

Wouldn't the world be a great place if everyone loved like Jesus said? Earlier this week you looked at some of the Ten Commandments. Most of them talked about things you should not do. But what about things you *should* do if you were trying really hard to love like Jesus said?

Match each commandment with the act that shows extra love.

___ 1. Do not take the Lord's name in vain.

___ 2. Keep the Lord's Day holy.

___ 3. Honor your father and mother.

___ 4. Do not kill.

___ 5. Do not steal.

___ 6. Do not lie.

A Hum a favorite hymn as you dress for Sunday Mass.

B Say something nice about a kid who is often put down.

C Every time you hear God's name misused, silently pray, "I love you, God."

D Do something nice for someone you sometimes feel like hitting!

E Ask your parents if you can help them with anything.

F Give away one of your favorite things.

Third Saturday of Lent — March 1

Today's Gospel: Luke 18:9-14

Jesus told this story. "Two men went up to the temple to pray, one a Pharisee and the other a tax collector. The Pharisee, standing by himself, prayed, 'God, I thank you that I am not like other people: thieves, rogues, adulterers, or even like this tax collector.' But the tax collector, standing far off, would not even look up to heaven, but was beating his breast and saying, 'God, be merciful to me, a sinner!' " (18:10-13)

Only one man's prayer pleased God that day. It was not the prayer of the Pharisee, who boasted of being better than others. It was the prayer of the tax collector who prayed with a humble heart.

1. What are some things that can make a kid think he or she is better than other kids? Circle them.

nice clothes	karate skills	big-screen TV
good grades	cool bike	athletic ability
deep faith	big house	humility
money	kindness	good looks
popularity	nice hair	latest computer games

*2. Now underline what **really** matters.*

3. Keeping in mind what really matters, write your own prayer to God.

Your Weekly Checkup

Keeping a Lenten resolution can be hard work. How hard have you worked on *yours* this week?

_____

Aesop told this fable about a farmer and two sons. The farmer was near death. He was afraid that his sons would not take care of the farm after he was gone. So he called his sons to his bedside. "My sons," he said, "I have buried a treasure in one of my fields." Those were his last words.

After his funeral, the sons hurried to the fields with their spades. They spent days and weeks digging. They dug here and there and everywhere. But they never did find a treasure. Had their father tricked them?

The answer came at harvest time. The new, freshly turned soil produced a *huge* harvest. That year both sons made much money from the harvest.

Can you think of a good moral for this story? Write it here.

_____

_____

_____

Who Wants to Be a Millionaire?

St. Katharine Drexel was born in 1858 to a very wealthy family in Philadelphia. She liked parties and having fun while growing up, but her parents also taught her about helping the needy. In fact, two times a week, they would invite poor people to dinner at their house.

St. Katharine grew up to be a caring and kind person. She founded a religious order of women called the Sisters of the Blessed Sacrament. She spent her fortune (more than 20 million dollars!) on starting schools and missions for Native and African Americans.

St. Katharine Drexel died in 1955 and was declared a saint in 2000. Her feast day is March 3.

Have you ever thought what you would do with a million dollars? It's fun to make plans, and most of us would probably think of what we could buy for ourselves. But this time, you must spend your million dollars on helping the poor. Write some ways you might do that.

_____

_____

_____

You may not have a million dollars to give away, but how could you help the poor today? Write your idea here. Then do it!

_____

Today's Gospel: John 4:43-54

"Unless you see signs and wonders you will not believe" (4:48).

One day when Jesus was in the town of Cana, a royal official from another town ran up to Jesus and started pleading with him to come home with him and cure his very ill son.

People were always asking Jesus for miracles to prove to them that he was the Son of God. So, Jesus questioned the man about his belief. But the man just kept asking for help. Finally, Jesus said, "Go; your son will live."

The man immediately left for home, which was long journey. The next day, his servants met him on the road to tell him that his son had started getting better at one in the afternoon the day before. That was the exact time Jesus had said, "Go; your son will live."

What did this man have that we all must have when we ask Jesus to help us? Solve this rebus to find out.

Working Line

Answer: ____ ____ ____ ____ ____.

Today's Gospel: John 5:1-16

The man answered, "Sir, I have no one to put me into the pool when the water is stirred up; and while I am making my way, someone else steps down ahead of me" (5:7).

In Jerusalem, there was a pool that people said had healing waters. Sometimes its waters would look very active, as if an angel of God were stirring them. When that happened, the first person into the pool got cured.

One Sabbath day, there at the pool, Jesus saw a man who had been disabled for thirty-eight years. He asked the man: "Do you want to be made well?" (5:6)

The man explained his problem of having no one to help him get into the water fast enough to be first. Jesus said: "Stand up, take your mat and walk" (5:8). At once the man was cured!

Some of the Jewish leaders started persecuting Jesus because he cured the man on a Sabbath, the day of rest. These leaders did not understand something Jesus understood. God *never* wants us to rest from love.

Decorate the cured man's mat with symbols of love.

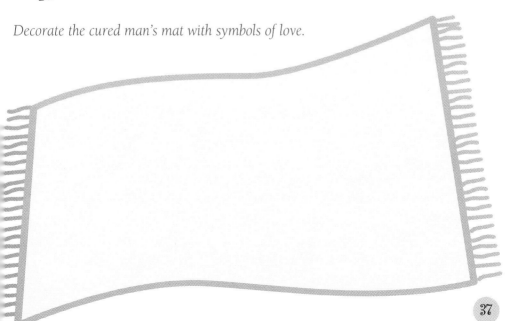

16 Fourth Wednesday of Lent — March 5

Today's Gospel: John 5:17-30

"Very truly, I tell you, the Son can do nothing on his own, but only what he sees the Father doing; for whatever the Father does, the Son does likewise" (5:19).

If today's Gospel were given a title, it would probably be "Like father, like son." Remember yesterday's Gospel? Some Jewish leaders got angry because Jesus cured a man on the Sabbath. Today, Jesus tells them why he did it.

In just a few words, Jesus tells them:
† God is his Father.
† His power to heal comes from his Father.
† His wish to help people comes from his Father.
† In all that he does, he imitates his Father.
† His Father loves and helps people every single day of the week.
† Jesus, too, loves and helps people every single day of the week.

1. Choose a parent or any other grown-up. Think of the good things that person does for family, friends, and neighbors. For example, maybe that person always listens. Or maybe that person usually cooks supper. List his or her good deeds here.

a)_____

b) _____

c) _____

d) _____

e)_____

f)_____

*2. Now put an **X** beside each good deed that you plan to do when you are grown up.*

*3. Which of these good deeds can you begin doing now? Put a second **X** beside each of those things.*

Today's Gospel: John 5:31-47

Jesus explains to unbelievers why they should believe in him. He says: "The works that the Father has given me to complete, the very works that I am doing, testify on my behalf that the Father has sent me" (5:36).

In other words, Jesus is saying:
† I have proof that the Father sent me.
† The proof is the good works that I do.

These good works included his miracles. Jesus worked many, many miracles during his life on earth.

From memory, can you name some of Jesus' good works, his miracles? List them here.

_____

_____

_____

Jesus worked miracles for **two big** reasons:

1. To help the sick, disabled, hungry, and troubled
2. To build up faith in everyone who saw his miracles

Which reason do you think was more important? Explain your answer.

_____

_____

_____

_____

Today's Gospel: John 7:1-2, 10, 25-30

He [Jesus] did not wish to go about in Judea because the Jews were looking for an opportunity to kill him (7:1).

Very important: The "Jews" means "some of the Jewish leaders." It does not mean "all Jews." Jesus himself was a Jew, and so were nearly all his friends and followers.

During the next two weeks of Lent, you will be hearing more about the Jews who wanted to kill Jesus. In today's Gospel, they tried to arrest Jesus, but "no one laid hands on him, because his hour had not yet come" (7:30). "His hour" means the hour of Jesus' death on the cross. He knew it was coming. But he knew it would come only in God's good time.

There is a right time for everything. On these clock faces, draw hands that show the right time for you to do each thing on any given Friday.

Wake up   Breakfast   Get to school   Lunch

Arrive home   Dinner   Evening   Prayers and bed

Today's Gospel: John 7:40-53

After Jesus preached one day, some in the crowd said, "This is the Messiah." But some asked, "Surely the Messiah does not come from Galilee, does he?" (7:41)

The land where Jesus lived was called Palestine. In the north it was called Galilee and in the south it was called Judea. Nazareth was in Galilee, and Jerusalem was in Judea. Some of Jesus' biggest enemies lived in Jerusalem. And they had closed their minds against him. They believed:

1. Galilee was a rough, wild place.
2. The people of Galilee did not properly understand God's law.
3. No great teacher or prophet would ever come from Galilee.

As a result, when God's own Son came to them, they had no idea who he was! Their bad example teaches us something. It teaches us to have open minds toward all people, no matter where they are from.

From these drawings, can you tell in what country each boy or girl probably lives? Put the name of the country under each figure. Choose from: France, South Africa, China, Mexico, or Israel.

Your Weekly Checkup

You are more than halfway through Lent! Is it getting easier or harder for you to keep your Lenten resolution? Or is it staying about the same?

_____

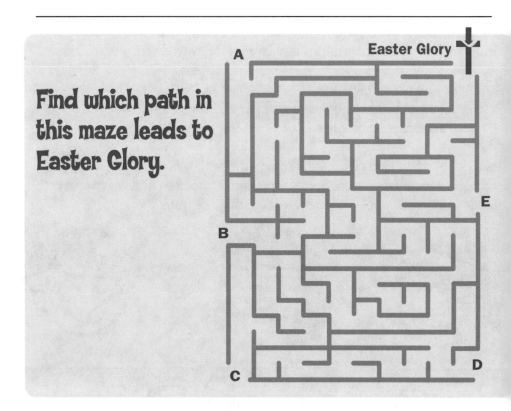

Find which path in this maze leads to Easter Glory.

Easter Grass

In the 1700s and 1800s, Germans settled in the empty steppes of Russia. (A steppe is a vast grassland.) These people became known as Russian Germans. They had some interesting holiday customs.

During Lent, for example, the mother of every family grew a pan of Easter grass. She told her children that, by Easter, the bunny would have a nice grassy place for his eggs. Of course, what the children found in this "nest" on Easter morning were colored eggs. Sound familiar?

Decorate With Easter Grass

Would you like to grow your own Easter grass? Watching it grow will remind you of how Jesus rose to new life after dying and being buried.

You can make a large pot of Easter grass to put in the center of your family's dinner table on Easter. Or, it's also fun to make small pots and put one by each person's plate at Easter dinner.

Ask your parents for permission to do this project and for any help you need.

Supplies

- an empty margarine tub or similar container
- plastic wrap
- potting soil
- ryegrass seeds or fast-growing whole-wheat berries
  (You can get these at a natural foods store.)
- water

Directions

1. Fill the container with soil.
2. Sprinkle the seeds on top.
3. Gently sprinkle the soil with water.
4. Cover the container with plastic wrap.
5. Place the container near a window, but not in direct sunlight.
6. Pull back plastic and sprinkle with fresh water daily. Replace plastic.
7. Watch the grass sprout within 4-5 days. When that happens, take away the plastic.
8. Keep watering the grass daily.
9. On Easter Sunday, decorate the container with Easter stickers or ribbon.
10. Lay colored eggs in the fresh grass.

Now you have a cheerful Easter decoration!

Today's Gospel: John 8:1-11

"Let anyone among you who is without sin be the first to throw a stone at her" (8:7).

Jesus reminded everyone today that nobody's perfect. Some Pharisees had dragged a sinful woman before Jesus, and reminded him that the law of Moses said she should be stoned to death for her sin.

After hearing Jesus' reply, who do you suppose was first to cast a stone? No one dared to do it because they all knew they were guilty of sins also.

Read the following list of sins you might commit sometimes. Check those you've been guilty of once in a while. Be honest!

DO YOU EVER...

___ lie or "stretch the truth" to get out of trouble?

___ sneak money from your mom's purse or dad's wallet?

___ talk back to parents or teachers?

___ pout if you don't get your way?

___ call people bad or hurtful names?

___ pretend you didn't hear when asked to help someone?

___ cheat on homework or tests?

___ break rules set by teachers or parents?

___ litter highways, streets, or classrooms?

If you checked a few items, don't get discouraged. Get busy! Ask Jesus to help you change, beginning today.

Today's Gospel: John 8:21-30

"Where I am going, you cannot come" (8:21).

The place was the temple in Jerusalem. The time was a big religious holiday. Jews from all over the land had come to worship.

"You are of this world, I am not of this world" (8:23).

To whom was Jesus speaking?

_____

If you guessed that Jesus was speaking to those Jews who still did not believe in him, you were right. Jesus never grew tired of trying to win people's hearts. He loved them, even if they didn't love him back.

"The one who sent me is with me; he has not left me alone, for I always do what is pleasing to him" (8:29).

About whom was Jesus speaking?_____

If you guessed that Jesus was talking **about** his Father in heaven, you were right. If we, like Jesus, always try to do what pleases the Father, we will never be alone. The Father will be with us—even during those times when we feel surrounded by enemies.

Jesus, I believe that you are the Father's Son. Help me to always do what is pleasing to him. Amen.

Today's Gospel: John 8:31-42

"If you continue in my word, you are truly my disciples; and you will know the truth, and the truth will set you free" (8:31).

This time, Jesus was talking to people who believed in him. They were really *trying* to understand him. Yet, why was Jesus promising to set them free? After all, they weren't slaves. They asked Jesus about this and he said, *"Very truly, I tell you, everyone who commits sin is a slave to sin"* (8:34).

How did that checklist on page 44 look after you finished it? Were there a few sins you could have *added* to the list? Sin, like slavery, keeps you from being really free.

The good news, though, is that you don't have to stay a slave. Jesus said: *"The slave does not have a permanent place in the household; the son has a place there forever. So if the Son makes you free, you will be free indeed"* (8:35-36).

Today's lesson is "Follow Jesus and you will be free!"

All but one of these items is a symbol of freedom. Cross out the one that is not.

Today's Gospel: John 8:51-59

"Very truly, I tell you, whoever keeps my word will never see death" (8:51).

In Jesus' time, one thing you never did was say something against Abraham. Abraham was revered as the father of the Jewish people.

So, the crowd reminded Jesus that Abraham had died. Did Jesus think he was greater than Abraham? When Jesus answered truthfully and said he *was*, the crowd got very angry and tried to stone him to death. But he got away and hid in the Temple.

*Do you ever get upset? Beside each item below, write **1** if that event would not bother you at all, **2** if it would bother you a little, and **3** if it would bother you a lot.*

___ Someone tries to steal your bike.

___ Someone yells, "Your mother's ugly."

___ Someone tries to burn your country's flag.

___ Someone toilet papers your house.

___ Someone starts punching your sister.

___ Someone puts you down for being the "wrong" nationality or color.

___ Someone yells, "You're an idiot!"

When we get upset, we need to ask ourselves, what if I'm wrong? What if there's something here that I don't understand?

Today's Gospel: John 10:31-42

The Jews took up stones again to stone him (10:31).

It's starting to feel a little dangerous walking with Jesus, isn't it? These stone-throwers were angry for the same old reason. Even though Jesus never lied to them, they couldn't get it through their heads that Jesus *was* God. Jesus was sent from the Father. He was one with the Father.

Sometimes you can see something only if you try looking at it in a different way. Hold up this page until the bottom edge is almost level with your eyes. Then you will be able to read an important message.

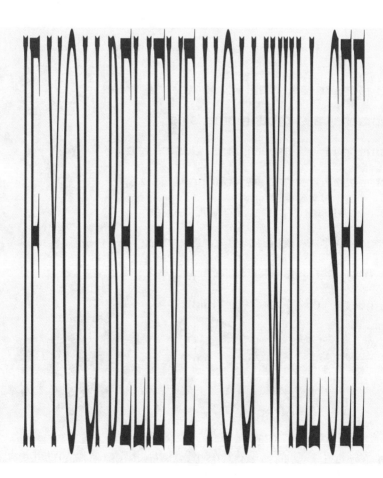

Today's Gospel: Luke 2:41-51

His mother said to him, "Child, why have you treated us like this? Look, your father and I have been searching for you in great anxiety" (2:48).

Today, an Amber Alert is issued as soon as the police know a child is missing. Within a short time, thousands of people are looking for the child.

But in Jesus' time, there were no Amber Alerts. There were no TVs, radios, telephones, internet, or other ways to alert people. When Jesus was missing, Mary and Joseph had to walk

from place to place, describing their son, and asking everyone they met if they had seen him. They were worried sick!

After three days, they found him in the Temple in Jerusalem. They were relieved to find him, but they didn't understand his explanation: *"Did you not know that I must be in my Father's house?"* (2:49)

What a confusing answer! St. Joseph was standing right there! As far as anyone knew, **he** was the father of Jesus. Although he was only Jesus' father on earth, Joseph loved Jesus very much and took good care of him.

*What do you do when you don't understand someone in your family? Cross out the things that you definitely should **not** do.*

Get angry	Call names	Listen attentively
Be respectful	Ask questions	Pout
Throw things	Lose your temper	Think things over

---

* The feast of St. Joseph (usually March 19th) is moved to the 15th this year because the 19th falls in Holy Week, when we focus on Jesus' suffering and death.

Walking with Jesus

Your Weekly Checkup

Remember way back on page 24 we talked about how we often compare people with animals? Someone is as wise as an owl, for example. Think about which animals *you* have been like this past week. *Be honest.* If you have *not* been very cheerful, say so: "I've been as cheerful as a bear with a bellyache!"

In keeping my Lenten resolution this week…

1. I've been as cheerful as _____.

2. I've been as faithful as _____.

3. I've been as hard-working as _____.

Palm Sunday

Palms remind us of Jesus entering Jerusalem with people waving palms to welcome him. Because the palm you bring home from church has been blessed, you must take special care of it.

If you want to braid it or make a cross with it, do it right away while the palm is green. Within days, it will turn yellow and get too brittle to braid or twist. Here's a simple way to make a Palm cross.

1. Begin with two palms, one for the vertical beam and a shorter one for the horizontal beam.

2. Place the shorter one across the longer one to form a cross.

3. Wind string or yarn around the center of the cross in every direction to secure the two beams.

4. Tie the ends of the string or yarn together in the back of the cross and cut off any tips that stick out.

Totem Poles

You have been learning a lot about Jesus' life on earth during your Lenten journey.

Use an animal's name to complete each of these sentences.

1. All his life, Jesus was as brave as

_____.

2. Jesus was as gentle as

_____.

3. Jesus was as mighty as

_____.

 Do you know what a totem pole is? It is a tall, thick wooden pole with different animal forms carved and painted on it. Native Americans of the Pacific Northwest have made totem poles for centuries. Each animal on the pole says something important about the family or clan who owns it. These are the animals that Native Americans usually put on their totem poles: wolves, beavers, bears, ravens, eagles, and whales.

Draw a "Jesus and Me" totem pole. Use the heads or forms of the three animals you used to describe yourself in this week's checkup and the animals you used to describe Jesus above.

Today's Gospel: John 12:1-11

Mary took a pound of costly perfume made of pure nard, anointed Jesus' feet and wiped them with her hair (12:3).

After the anointing, Judas criticized Mary and asked why the perfume had not been sold and the money given to the poor. (He really wanted the money for himself.) Mary was showing her love for Jesus. She was right. Judas was wrong. Mary was a true disciple of Jesus. Judas was a false disciple.

*Mark each quality in this list with either a **T** for True disciple or an **F** for False disciple. Then find the word in the Word Search.*

disloyal	greedy	joyful	mean
foolish	helpful	kind	polite
giving	humble	lazy	proud

G	R	M	G	E	L	B	M	U	H
R	R	M	G	G	N	T	C	P	L
L	F	V	R	A	I	Q	P	A	M
L	G	P	E	E	R	V	Y	Q	H
P	U	M	E	X	T	O	I	E	X
D	Y	F	D	P	L	I	L	N	X
N	Z	X	Y	S	R	P	L	Y	G
I	A	K	I	O	F	O	J	O	K
K	L	D	K	U	J	H	U	N	P
F	O	O	L	I	S	H	D	D	W

* The feast of St. Patrick (usually March 17th) is not celebrated this year since the 17th falls in Holy Week, whe we focus on Jesus' suffering and death.

Today's Gospel: John 13:21-33, 36-38

Peter said to Jesus, "Lord,...I will lay down my life for you." Jesus answered, "Will you lay down your life for me? Very truly, I tell you, before the cock crows, you will have denied me three times" (13:36-38).

Peter
Quick, brash
jumping, running, following
He trails after Jesus.
Shadow

This poem compares Peter to Jesus' shadow. Even though Peter denied knowing Jesus, he stuck to Jesus like a shadow. He watched where they took Jesus. He watched what they did with him. He loved Jesus dearly, and he had to know.

Now it's your turn. Think about the kind of friend Jesus was to Peter (or Jesus is to you) and write a poem about it. Write your poem on the lines provided. Follow the steps given for each line.

Line 1: List two words that describe Jesus as a friend.
Line 2: List three words ending in *ing* that also tell about Jesus as a friend.
Line 3. Write one four-word sentence about Jesus.
Line 4: Write one word to sum up the kind of friend Jesus is.

Jesus

_____ , _____

_____ , _____ , _____

_____ _____ _____ _____.

_____

Today's Gospel: Matthew 26:14-25

Jesus said to the twelve, "Truly I tell you, one of you will betray me." One by one each asked, "Surely not I, Lord?" When Judas asked the question, Jesus replied, "You have said so" (26:20-22, 25).

Think of all that Jesus has done for you so that you might know and feel his love. Think of how you might return his friendship.

Inside this crown of thorns, draw a few symbols of Jesus' love for you, such as a cross, three nails, grapes, wheat, or a fiery heart. Then slowly pray the Act of Love below.

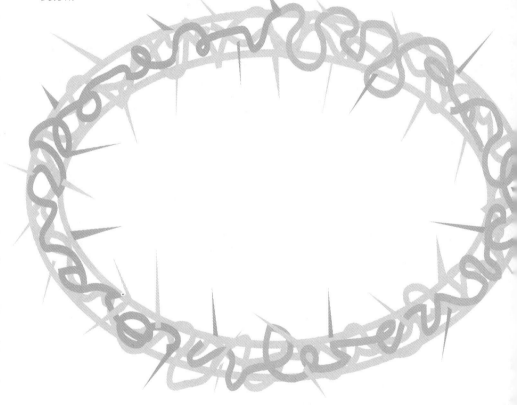

My God, I love you above all things,
with my whole heart and soul,
because you are all-good and worthy of all love.
I love my neighbor as myself for love of you.
I forgive all who have injured me
and ask pardon of all whom I have injured. Amen.

Today's Gospel: John 13:1-15

Jesus knew that his hour had come to depart from this world and go to the Father. Having loved his own who were in the world, he loved them to the end....[He] got up from the table, took off his outer robe, and tied a towel around himself. Then he poured water into a basin and began to wash the disciples' feet (13:1, 4-5).

What would you do if you had only one more day to live? Some think of all the fun they would cram into their last day. Others think of all the people they would want to see or talk with—all the people they would tell "I love you" or "I'm sorry."

Jesus knew when it was his last day to live on this earth. He chose to spend it with his disciples and to show them that he loved them by washing their feet—a sign of great respect and affection in those days.

If Jesus could, he would wash your feet, too, because he loves and respects you as his disciple today.

Draw your own face on the child whose feet Jesus is washing.

Today's Gospel: John 18:1—19:42

Walk with Jesus on his way to Calvary today. Write your own short prayer after each station. The first is done for you.

1. Pilate sentences Jesus to death.
Lord, you are so brave. Help me to be brave enough to follow you always.

2. Soldiers give Jesus a heavy cross to carry.

3. Jesus falls the first time.

4. Jesus meets his mother along the road.

5. Soldiers order Simon of Cyrene to help Jesus with his cross.

6. Veronica wipes Jesus' face with a cloth.

7. Jesus falls a second time.

8. Jesus meets a group of women weeping for him.

9. Jesus falls a third time.

10. Soldiers strip Jesus of his clothes.

11. Soldiers nail Jesus to the cross.

12. Jesus dies on the cross.

13. Jesus' friends take his body down from the cross.

14. Jesus' friends lay his body in a tomb.

Holy Saturday—
March 22

Today's Gospel: Matthew 28:1-10

After the Sabbath, as the first day of the week was dawning, Mary Magdalene and the other Mary went to see the tomb. And suddenly there was a great earthquake; for an angel of the Lord, descending from heaven, came and rolled back the stone and sat on it. His appearance was like lightning, and his clothing white as snow. For fear of him the guards shook and became like dead men (28:1-4).

Using a Bible, read the entire Gospel for today. Imagine you are one of the men or women at Jesus' tomb today and that your parents or some good friends live in a distant city.

Write them a letter about what you saw and heard.

Dear_____,

_____

_____

_____

_____

_____

_____

_____

_____

_____

_____

_____

Love,

_____

Victory Banner

Pictures of the risen Jesus often show him carrying a victory banner. It has a big cross on it. There are many different ways to draw a cross. These are just a few examples:

Also, there are two popular symbols for victory:

Design a victory banner for Jesus using any of these symbols or ones that you create yourself. The banner should show that Jesus has defeated sin and death through his death and resurrection.

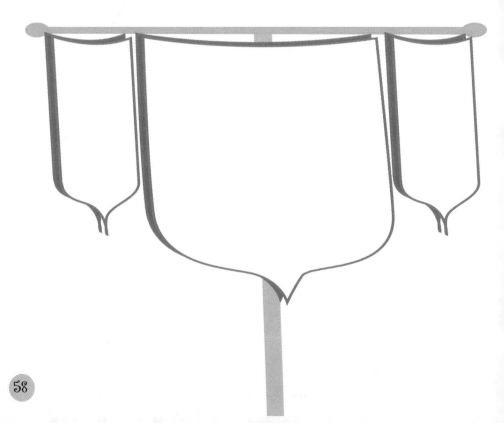

Easter Butterflies

When a caterpillar spins a cocoon around itself, it appears to die. Have you ever seen a cocoon? It looks gray, dead, and lifeless.

Can you imagine the surprise of the very first human being who ever watched a beautiful butterfly burst out of its cocoon? These surprising creatures are good symbols of Jesus' resurrection to new life.

Decorate this butterfly with pretty designs that suggest joy, hope, and new life.

Easter Sunday—
March 23

Today's Gospel: John 20:1-9

Then the other disciple, who reached the tomb first, also went in, and he saw and believed; for as yet they did not understand the scripture, that he must rise from the dead (8-9).

Peter and John still did not understand that Jesus' mission was to conquer sin and death. And he did that through his death and resurrection. Even as close as they had been to Jesus, they just couldn't clearly see and understand. Maybe they were too close to the truth to see it.

What do you think this is? Write your guess here.

_____

Try this!

Find ten magazines with big pictures on their covers. Turn the magazines face down. Mix them up. Close your eyes and pick up a magazine. Keep your eyes closed as you turn the magazine over. Keep it so close to your face that your nose touches the front cover. Then, without moving the magazine *at all*, open your eyes, and guess what is on the cover.

This will be harder to do than you think! If you think it's easy, though, try doing the same thing with a stack of magazine covers you have never seen before. Have another person get them ready for you.

Keep Walking with Jesus

"Listen! I am standing at the door, knocking; if you hear my voice and open the door, I will come in to you and eat with you, and you with me" (Revelation 3:20).

Just because Lent is over doesn't mean you should stop walking with Jesus every day. Here is a good way to do that.

Every night before you go to bed, read just a paragraph or two from the Gospels. Begin with *The Gospel According to Mark*. It is the shortest Gospel and the easiest one to understand.

After reading a short section, turn off the lights and talk over with Jesus what you have read. Tell him what you think the passage means. If it makes you feel a little happy or a little sad or even a little confused, tell him about it. If the passage reminds you of something you need to ask for, then ask. End by praying the Our Father.

After you finish Mark's Gospel, go on to Luke's, then Matthew's, then John's. In this way, you can continue to walk with Jesus all year long.

Remember, Jesus is a real person, not a character in a storybook! Reading from the Gospels each day is like letting Jesus inside your heart to feed your soul. You'll never find a better friend than the one Jesus wants to be for you.

He Is Risen! Alleluia!

Easter is here and the mood in church has changed dramatically. We've moved from purple to white vestments. We sing out Alleluias with gusto. Churches are filled with beautiful Easter lilies, colorful banners, and other signs of celebration.

After all, this is the greatest feast of the year for Christians. If Jesus had not suffered, died, and risen, there would be no Christians anywhere. No one would have believed he was the Son of God.

Read John 20:19-31. This is the Gospel for the first Sunday *after* Easter. It tells the story of the first time Jesus appeared to his disciples after he had risen from the dead. Can you imagine an experience like that?

Write what you think your reaction would have been. What would you have said to Jesus?

_____

_____

_____

_____

_____

_____

_____

_____

Answers to Activities

Page 7: 1, 5, 7, 8 = Almsgiving. 2, 6, 10, 12 = Praying. 3, 4, 9, 11 = Fasting.

Page 8:

F	M	C	H	E	A	T	K	P
V	S	K	E	R	Y	C	N	D
E	K	Q	I	H	A	V	I	C
S	I	B	L	B	U	S	N	T
R	P	U	K	B	O	R	N	E
U	M	L	M	B	W	R	T	N
C	A	L	E	V	G	A	R	B
T	S	V	T	H	G	I	F	L
Q	S	L	S	T	E	A	L	N

Page 9: Those who are well do not need a doctor. Only sick people do. I have come not to call good people but to call sinners.

Page 11: Note: Answers to 1 and 2 could be switched and still be correct.
1=L; 2=E; 3=F; 4=I; 5=C; 6=A; 7=K; 8=D; 9=J; 10=G; 11=H; 12=B

Page 15: 1. bread; 2. stone; 3. fish; 4. snake.

Page 16: 1. kill; 2. hurt; 3. yank; 4. dis; 5. hate; 6. bother; 7. knock or sock; 8. slug or mug; 9. hit; 10. fight; 11. kick; 12. pester.

Page 19: 1, 3, 4, 7, 10=Peter Damian. 2, 5, 6, 8, 9=Peter the Apostle

Page 22: C

Page 23: day, sores, table, Abraham, heaven, up, things, divide, other, brothers, them, Moses, prophets, dead

Page 24: 1. bat; 2. peacock; 3. toad; 4. bee; 5. elephant; 6. horse; 7. goose; 8. mule; 9. snake in the grass; 10. ox

Page 25:
1, 3=Y; 2, 4, 5=O
The father represents God the Father.

Page 26: E.

Page 27: D

Page 28: He passed right through the midst of them and went on his way.

Page 29: 77 times; Sweet 16; Terrible 2s; Lucky 7 or 11; Unlucky 13; A perfect 10; Loneliest number=1

Page 30: 1=C; 2=E; 3=F; 4=B; 5=D; 6=A

Page 32: 1=C; 2=A; 3=E; 4=D; 5=F; 6=B

Page 36: LEAF+RAIN-EAR+EGG-LEG-N+THREE+L-G-REEL=FAITH

Page 41: Top row: Mexico, China, France. Bottom row: Israel, South Africa.

Page 42: Correct path is C.

Page 46: A turkey is not a symbol of freedom.

Page 48: If you believe, you will see.

Page 52:

G	R	M	G	E	L	B	M	U	H
R	R	M	G	G	N	T	C	P	L
L	F	V	R	A	I	Q	P	A	M
L	G	P	E	E	R	V	Y	Q	H
P	U	M	E	X	T	O	I	E	X
D	Y	F	D	P	L	I	L	N	X
N	Z	X	Y	S	R	P	L	Y	G
I	A	K	I	O	F	O	J	O	K
K	L	D	K	U	J	H	U	N	P
F	O	O	L	I	S	H	D	D	W

Page 60: